When School
—— Is a ——
Struggle

Curt Dudley·Marling

SCHOLASTIC

Scholastic Canada Ltd.
123 Newkirk Road, Richmond Hill, Ontario, Canada L4C 3G5

Scholastic Inc.
730 Broadway, New York, NY 10003, USA

Ashton Scholastic Limited
Private Bag 1, Penrose, Auckland , New Zealand

Ashton Scholastic Pty Limited
PO Box 579, Gosford, NSW, 2250, Australia

Scholastic Publications Ltd.
Holly Walk, Leamington Spa, Warwickshire CV32 4LS, England

Cover photo © Garry Briand/First Light

Canadian Cataloguing in Publication Data

Dudley-Marling, Curt
  When school is a struggle

ISBN 0-590-73609-4

1. Learning, Psychology of. I. Title.

LB1051.D83 1990   370.15   C90-095724-7

Contents

To Anne, my "too too girl."

Your too thin legs make me giggle.
Your too loud voice makes me cringe.
Your too small teeth put a smile on my face.
Your too messy room makes me growl.
Your too brown eyes make me warm inside.
Your too sad days make me cry.
Up —
           or down,
You're my too too girl,
And I love you too too much.

Prologue

During my undergraduate years at the University of Cincinnati I was never quite sure what I would do with the psychology major I was working on, but a chance summer job in 1969 changed that. I had just completed my Red Cross Water Safety Instructor course and was looking for a job at a swimming pool. I didn't have much luck until one day I got a call from Rick Spiegle, the director of Camp Courageous, a camp for retarded children near Toledo, Ohio. Camp was starting in just a few weeks and someone he had hired earlier had had a change of mind, leaving him without anyone to run the swimming program. Would I be interested? I didn't know anything about retarded children, but I did need a job. I leaped at the chance.

My experience at Camp Courageous changed me. I loved it! Maybe, I decided, helping handicapped children would be something I could do for a living. Toward the end of the summer I wrote to the special education department at the University of Cincinnati about becoming a special education teacher. Within two weeks I received a reply from Connie Madsen, a professor in special education there. With her encouragement I finished my B.A. in psychology, then enrolled in a special education Masters program. Connie continued to assist and support my career moves until she died a few years ago. I lost a dear friend then, as did many others whose lives she had touched.

My first teaching job took me to Fair Acres School in Hamilton, Ohio, to work with a group of moderately and severly retarded children. Phil Estes, the principal at Fair Acres, inspired Fred Valerius, Bobbi Goist and the rest of us there to care deeply about our students. We wanted desperately to help them, to protect them from the harsh realities of daily life. I remember how some of my college friends envied me because I had chosen such a socially relevant career. Most of us were, after all, children of the '60's.

At Fair Acres I was committed to helping children to whom I felt fate had been unkind. I believed deeply in what I was doing. Yet at the same time I wasn't altogether happy with the ways I was doing it.

Much of what I had been taught about mentally retarded children stressed that they needed to learns skills, usually rote skills, to prepare them for independent or semi-independent lives as adults. One of my professors had told us that most mentally retarded children would never be able to learn anything except what she called "splinter" skills.

So I taught my students skills. I didn't teach them to talk, I taught them the skills of labeling pictures and repeating sentences. I didn't teach them to run and play, I taught them the skills of walking a balance beam and throwing beanbags through holes in targets. I was vaguely unhappy about it all, but I didn't know what else to do. I did start to fill bigger and bigger chunks of the school days with recesses, field trips and unplanned walks around town which, in retrospect, probably left more positive effects on the children than my teaching of specific skills. But the whole experience made me feel somehow inadequate as a teacher.

As a possible way out of my discontent I decided to try some additional professional education. In 1973 I took a language development course at the University of Cincinnati from Richard Kretschmer, whom I consider the best teacher I ever had. I still remember that whole course as a liberating experience.

Led by Noam Chomsky, language theorists had long recognized the inadequacies of the behavioral theories that had dominated my previous courses in psychology and special education. Dr. Kretschmer acquainted me with their work, and with their attempts to replace those inadequate theories with better ones. I discovered, among other things, that there were already many new ways being suggested for encouraging language learning in the classroom, a point of immediate practical importance to me.

As I began to reject my behavioral approach to language teaching, I began to have serious doubts about all the educational methods I'd ever been taught. I started to read Piaget, Vygotsky, Bruner, Smith and others. As I read and reflected, a view of learning and teaching evolved within me that was very different from what I'd learned in school myself. I gradually came to believe that children (and adults) learn to read, write, talk and think by holistic practice, not through the drill of hierarchies of skills and subskills. I became particularly interested in literacy, especially in what is now often called a "whole language" view of literacy and literacy learning.

In 1976 I moved to Green Bay, Wisconsin, to teach children with learning disabilities. But even though I learned a lot from my students, and through the implementation of some new teaching practices, my professional questions didn't stop. I wanted to know much more about teaching and learning. So in 1978 I returned to school to pursue a doctorate at the University of Wisconsin.

My studies in linguistics affected me most, I think. More and more I was awed by the incredible complexity of language and, by implication, the remarkable achievements of language learners. More and more I began to focus on an understanding of the role of context in language learning and language use. In fact, I came to realize that context plays a large role in all human learning.

In 1981 I took a teaching position at the University of Colorado at Denver, where I worked closely with Lynn Rhodes, an outstanding teacher, scholar and friend. There I learned a great deal more about literacy. In particular I began to understand that all I already knew about oral language and oral language learning applied to reading and writing as well.

In 1985 I moved to York University in Toronto. Here a number of colleagues, especially Lous Heshusius, influenced me to consider the basic philosophical and pedagogical assumptions underlying my ideas. I began to see that what I was working on was not just a new approach to teaching reading, writing and oral language, but a basic philosophy about human knowledge and human learning. I began to see that my discomfort with what I had been taught about teaching didn't indicate a mere methodological quibble, but a basic difference in world views.

Traditional teaching methods are rooted in a world view that can be traced back to the philosophy of Descartes and Locke and some of the Greek philosophers, and to the science of Newton. The modern version of this world view has dominated Western society for the last 400 years. These great thinkers influenced us to separate mind and body, body and soul, and to see ourselves as part of an orderly, highly predictable universe that exists regardless of our place in it. We came to see our world as a mathematically precise machine, one we could describe and understand by searching for fundamental building blocks and demonstrable causes and effects. And although modern thinkers of many stripes — including theoretical physics scholars — are now putting profound questions to this model of thinking, the effects of it persist in many layers of our culture. We still continue to search for simple causes and technological cures for the economic, envionmental and social problems that plague modern society.

"Behaviorism" is a catchword for the set of commonly held assumptions about teaching and learning that arose from the influence of Descartes and Newton. It would have us believe that we can quantify children's learning, and sort and rank living human beings along scales of performance and ability. Behaviorists think it's possible to reduce learning and teaching to sequences of fundamental building blocks or skills. They act as if human emotion can be separated from the educational decision-making process. They believe that they can identify causes of children's learning problems and prescribe specific remedies. After all, according to Newton, if the (human) machine is broken, then it can be fixed.

But these assumptions aren't facts. They are postulates

that uphold a specific world view. They are glasses through which we choose to see the world. What often fools us is that so many people seem to wear the same glasses.

My own professional development has made me see that this old view of the world is increasingly being questioned, by many and varied groups of people. Quantum mechanics and new mathematical theories have leapfrogged the old Newtonian model. Modern philosophers are revisiting Descartes and Locke and finding them wanting. New views of the world are emerging. We are coming to see our world less in terms of basic building blocks and simple causes and effects, and more in terms of dynamic, complex, interacting systems. We are beginning to understand, for example, that our economic, environmental and social woes are interrelated and can be understood only within the infinitely complex contexts in which they occur.

When I think back on my undergraduate years and my early years of teaching, I realize how differently I see the world now. My vague worries then about failing my students have been replaced by a much richer understanding of how they can be productive learners. I've come to believe that the assumptions underlying behaviorism are fundamentally flawed. And there's real urgency in that conclusion, because the old world view has seriously inhibiting consequences for students whose education has been and is being guided by it.

For a long time I understood all this only at an intellectual and professional level. But then I became a parent as well, and new human dimensions were added by my daughter Anne's struggles in first grade. Of course I knew that some children don't do well academically. My career had been devoted to helping children who struggle in school. But this wasn't *some* child. This was our little girl. I hoped and prayed that she would catch on and that school wouldn't become a permanent struggle for her. I did all I could to help her but, despite all that I know about reading and writing, I'm her parent, not her teacher.

I worried about how her teachers would respond to her. Would they see her as a learner or as a learning problem? I knew from the research and from my own experience that many teachers still respond to reading problems by focusing on skills. They set out to teach children *how* to read and write, often by means of artificial and lifeless chunks of text, instead of encouraging them to read and write real texts. For the old model that approach is appropriate, but for the new way of thinking, it isn't. I honestly believe that this standard kind of approach doesn't help, and may make matters worse.

But my concern was no longer the objective concern of an academic. The whole question was now relevant to my Anne. For her sake, and for others like her, I felt the time had come to present a concrete alternative to educators of children who struggle. And so this book was born.

While it isn't a case study of my daughter, writing it has given me the opportunity to confront my own feelings about her early struggles in school. It expresses my fears and my hopes for all children who don't do well in school. At heart I'm committed to those children, as I was to the handicapped children in Camp Courageous more than two decades ago. I still see myself as a special educator committed to helping children for whom school can be an inhospitable place. So this book is written for my daughter Anne, and for all those children who sometimes struggle in school.

Why do children fail?

Every morning at 6:30 my two-and-a-half-year-old son Ian bellows from the crib in his bedroom, "MAAA! MAAA!" This is his not-so-subtle announcement that he wants to be picked up out of his crib. Ian still hasn't learned to climb out by himself, for which we're grateful. His sister learned to climb out of her crib when she was about ten months old, and we rather wished she hadn't. Ian also learned to talk much later than Anne. But don't feel too sorry for Ian; he does many things very well. He was able to carry a tune when he was only nine months. His sister couldn't do that until she was six *years*. And Ian already catches and hits a ball better than she does.

Most of us are comfortable with these kinds of developmental differences. We realize that variation is a normal part of human development. We take comfort in the fact that such differences aren't necessarily permanent. A late walker, for example, still might become a fine athlete.

Why then do we expect developmental differences to disappear when children enter school? We become increasingly concerned, even alarmed, when our children's school work is "below average." Developmental differences which we consider normal in two-year-olds become intolerable in eight-year-olds.

These concerns are rooted in basic behavioral beliefs about the nature of school learning. Most schools quantify children's learning, and rank students on a bell curve according to their mastery of a sequence of skills. From this perspective, developmental differences are seen as deficiencies (which are bad) rather than instances of normal variation (which aren't bad). Schools respond to children's difficulties with a flurry of testing and meetings. In extreme cases, special programming is provided, perhaps with full-time or part-time placement in a special class. And how can parents not respond to all of this with a mixture of anxiety and anguish?

I'm not suggesting that parents and teachers shouldn't feel concerned if their children aren't doing well in school. Of course they should. But there's an important question I think we have to consider: how do we respond to those children who struggle in school, and how does our response affect their genuine learning? In other words, do we ourselves inadvertently *discourage* meaningful learning in some children? Do we help cause our own children to fail through our efforts to help them? And if so, how does this happen?

Tunnel vision

The behavioral perspective sees human knowledge and learning as a collection of discrete abilities arranged in a fairly invariable scope and sequence. Children's progress is measured by comparing their growth to some absolute (adult) standard — that is, to some previously defined sequence of skills. Viewed this way, children's struggles are seen in terms of deficits. We test to see what they can't do, or don't do well, then focus our instruction on these deficits.

I see real trouble in this approach, because when we look at children this way we risk being afflicted with tunnel vision. It blinds us to their marvelous accomplishments and focusses our attention instead on their difficulties, on what they cannot do. It affects how we interact with them and how we teach them. Instead of being loving teachers and parents we become mechanics, intent on making our children better, on "fixing" them.

> My wife and I once ate at a restaurant in Milwaukee. The waitress had a large pimple on the end of her nose. I recall having great difficulty drawing my attention away from that pimple. To this day the only thing I can remember about the restaurant, the meal or the waitress is that large pimple on the end of her nose.

I suppose it's human nature to notice people's unusual physical characteristics. In Steve Martin's movie *Roxanne,* one of the veteran firefighters warns a newcomer that when he meets the chief (Steve Martin), he won't be able to draw his attention away from the chief's enormous nose, no matter how hard he tries.

Human nature or not, I find this tendency disturbing. How are we affected when we allow our attention to be drawn to insignificant differences in people? What do we lose when we notice foremost an unimportant aspect of a human being? I'm afraid we risk overlooking some of the fine qualities people have. By seeing first what they are not (pretty, successful, athletic, slim), we may miss seeing what they really are (warm, caring, funny).

> When I was studying to become a teacher I did a four-week internship at a clinic where children were tested to determine their eligibility for a special school for children with learning disabilities. While I was administering several tests to a young boy, Clark, it began to snow. Soon Clark was paying more attention to the snow outside the window than to our tests. My attention was also drawn to the snow outside, but nevertheless I added Clark's distractibility to the other "evidence" that he had a learning disability.

> Clark had been referred to the clinic because someone suspected he had a learning problem. I immediately tunnel-visioned myself. Already convinced that he had a learning problem, I set myself to find it. When I saw him looking out the window at the snow I didn't see the normal, healthy curiosity of a nine-year-old boy, I saw deviant behavior. I saw a learning disability. I allowed my expectations of what I thought learning disabled children were like to dictate how I saw one individual boy. I became quick to interpret his behavior as deviant, and unwilling to give him the benefit of the doubt. I looked out the window because I was curious; he looked out the window because he was distractible. I can only wonder now how my attitude affected his behavior towards me that day, and mine towards him.

I'm still dismayed at how I handled that situation almost 20 years ago. I'd be a bit less anxious today if I knew we don't do that kind of thing anymore. But I'm afraid I still see a lot of it going on. People still label students in terms of what they see as learning or behavior problems, which only forces the attention of both teachers and parents onto what's *wrong* with their children, and encourages them to interpret the students' behavior in terms of those problems. Occasional inattentiveness, anger or restlessness is common to all school-age children. But when children who don't do well in school exhibit these behaviors, we consider them evidence that there is a (serious!) problem.

> When I entered one special education classroom, six students were seated in front of the teacher. The group was brainstorming writing topics, and the teacher wrote their ideas on the chalkboard as they spoke. When they finished brainstorming, the teacher introduced tracking sheets. She told the group to record what they'd done with their writing that day and what they expected they'd be doing the next.
>
> *Teacher:* Today we brainstormed topics [she wrote *brainstorm topics* on the chalkboard]. When you go back to your desks you're going to select a topic [she wrote *select a topic*], and then we're going to start writing [she wrote *start writing*]. Now who can tell me what we're going to do tomorrow?
>
> *Paul:* Start writing.
>
> *Teacher:* No, we started writing today. What are we going to do tomorrow?
>
> No one spoke. The students appeared visibly puzzled.
>
> *Teacher:* What are we going to do tomorrow? Today we started to write. Tomorrow we're going to . . . ?
>
> *Margaret:* Continue —
>
> *Teacher* [cutting Margaret off]: Yes, we're going to continue writing what we started writing today.
>
> At this point she sent the students back to their seats. When they were all seated, she walked over to me and said, "That was like pulling teeth."

What was going on here? When Paul responded to the teacher's question by answering, "Start writing," she apparently believed he meant that tomorrow they would start writing *for the first time.* The students' puzzlement suggested to me that they thought he meant that tomorrow they would start writing *again,* which was a reasonable answer. Yet the teacher concluded from the conversation that these students were unable to come up with the right answer.

I suppose that this confusion could be dismissed as a simple misunderstanding. Unfortunately, I see the same sort of thing happening frequently in special education classes. Here is another example:

> *Teacher:* What are you doing in the picture?
>
> *Student:* Skating.
>
> *Teacher:* Will you tell me a sentence about it?
>
> *Student:* I go skating.
>
> *Teacher:* Where?
>
> *Student:* In the Mill Pond.
>
> *Teacher:* In the Mill Pond? Are you right in the Mill Pond?
>
> *Student:* Yeah. No.
>
> *Teacher:* No. [Laughs] Where are you?
>
> *Student:* Skating.
>
> *Teacher:* Yes, but you're not in the Mill Pond. You'd be all wet if you were in it. Where are you?
>
> *Student:* Skating, I think. I don't know. Icing, I think.
>
> *Teacher:* Sometimes we say, "Skating *at* the Mill Pond."
>
> *Student:* Yeah.

This common classroom incident simply left the teacher frustrated and the student confused about what his teacher expected from him. I'm frustrated myself when I consider how often I see special education teachers getting caught in similar situations. I think it's the effect of tunnel vision, which entices us to believe that the speech of students we think have learning problems is insufficiently explicit. But is it really so? I'm almost certain that if an academically able student had said that tomorrow he was going to "start writing" or that she had been skating "in the Mill Pond" the teacher wouldn't even have noticed.

One of my York University colleagues, Dennis Searle, once suggested to me that when misunderstandings arise between teachers and academically successful students, teachers are willing to believe that the blame for the confusion rests with them and not their students. When Dennis was in high school he was a very good student and, if he looked confused while a teacher was lecturing, the teacher would often stop and ask him what the problem was, how had he or she confused him? Based on my own experiences, I wonder if Dennis's teachers would have accepted any personal responsibility for the confusion of less successful students.

I'm afraid that many teachers automatically assume student incompetence when they are working with children who don't always do well in school. This assumption leads them to see and hear the students in expected ways. They see incompetence because they expect to see it. And, as in the example of the teacher for whom teaching was "like pulling teeth," teachers act on these assumptions, often to the detriment of the students.

Several years ago Lynn Rhodes and I studied the reading development of six boys and girls in a primary level learning disability class. One of the girls, Maxine, moved to a new school in the middle of the year, but we were given permission to follow her. This also gave us the opportunity to see how Maxine reacted to both her old and her new teachers, who practiced very different approaches to reading instruction. We observed, for instance, how both teachers reacted to Maxine's oral reading errors. The first teacher almost always responded by saying nothing. Maxine would usually correct her errors if her reading didn't make sense or, if it did make sense, she would read on. The second teacher always responded by immediately correcting any errors.

It's likely that these two teachers developed very different perceptions of Maxine's abilities. The second teacher, busy as she was correcting mistakes, learned nothing about Maxine's ability to self-correct. She didn't learn that reading for meaning was important to Maxine and that, when what Maxine was reading didn't make sense to her, she attempted to correct herself. This teacher's tendency to correct Maxine's miscues immediately masked much of what the student actually knew about reading. The teacher learned only how Maxine read words, not what strategies she used to deal with words in context.

The first teacher, by contrast, didn't hurry to correct Maxine's oral reading errors. She was less concerned with isolated skills and subskills (in this case, getting the words right) than with the whole of reading — that is, making sense of print. Because of her focus on the whole of what readers do, she learned much more about what Maxine did in the process of reading.

Teacher behaviors can directly affect our perception of a student's performance. They can inadvertently reinforce our perceptions of good and poor students by preventing us from discovering what those students really know.

I'm not suggesting that students who don't do well in school really have no problems at all, or that their struggles are solely the result of adult expectations. What I do want to suggest is that teachers and parents be careful about concluding that their children suffer from some sort of general incompetence just because they don't always do well in school. A negative judgment of that kind will affect how we treat students who fall behind and, soon enough, will affect even the children's own perceptions of themselves as learners and as people.

Challenge . . . or something else

The behavioral model of teaching has dominated the education of students for whom school is a struggle. It has influenced many special education teachers to provide instruction that focusses on learning how instead of doing. Those teachers don't ask children to read and write and do math, but instead require endless exercises that are supposed to lead to reading, writing and math. Their students may get better at the isolated skills that are assumed to be necessary for learning those things, but without ample opportunities to use real reading, writing and mathematics to fulfill their personal needs, they won't learn any more than that.

Why are so many people — teachers and parents — attracted to the behavioral approach for students who don't do well in school? I think it's mostly because they lack faith that their charges can learn like other children. And I believe that this lack of faith itself will guarantee that some students won't learn.

One day at the local park I overheard one of the mothers complaining about a teacher at my daughter's school. In this mother's view, the teacher didn't "challenge students who need challenging."

On my way home from the park I kept wondering what the mother meant. I wished that I'd asked her what the teacher hadn't done that she wanted her to do. She was probably worried that the work at school was too easy for her son and afraid that he would become bored. I suppose she meant that she wanted harder work for her boy.

I have a lot of sympathy for what that mother said. I agree that her son needs to be challenged if he's going to learn in school. He needs to have his intellectual resources stretched and, in the process, expand his intellect. He needs to learn through solving problems, overcoming obstacles and dealing with uncertainties. So the element of "challenge" in her observation didn't bother me one bit. But she said that her son's teacher didn't "challenge students who need challenging." What bothered me was that clearly, in her view, some students need to be challenged while others need something else.

Many people, like this mother, believe that only some students need to be challenged — the more academically capable ones, like her son. Even a cursory look at enrichment and gifted programs will reveal a lot more emphasis on logical reasoning and problem solving than is offered in regular classrooms. The clear implication is that these areas are important to bright students but not quite so important to those students who are presumed to be less able. They need to focus their attention on learning the basics instead.

Some people will argue that for academically less successful students the basics are challenging enough, but I don't think that's what is meant when educators talk about challenging children. I think they really believe that we should teach bright students by encouraging them to use higher level thinking skills, while students we perceive as less able need to be more concerned with basic skills and rote learning, at least for the time being.

A superintendent of special education in a school district near Toronto recently told her staff that the active, holistic approach to education being emphasized in her district was not appropriate for learning disabled students. Those children would benefit more from a program of basic skills instruction. A lot of educators agree with this conclusion. As a result, in general, instruction for lower achievers is much more likely to emphasize so-called basic skills and subskills than the instruction provided for higher achievers.

It's hard to break loose from the conclusion that some students don't need to be challenged. Surrounded as we are by behaviorist notions, it's hard to retain our faith in the natural ability of all children to learn. We're constantly tempted to conclude that some children learn differently. We even worry that challenging less successful students will do them harm by frustrating them. So some students get challenged while others get something else. The question is, is that something else really in the best interest of the students for whom it's prescribed?

A vicious circle

The teacher pointed to the letter *c* and Carolyn said "ka." The teacher then pointed to the *a* and Carolyn said "ah." When she pointed to the *t*, Carolyn said "tuh." Then the teacher said, "Put it all together now," and Carolyn said, "Ka—ah—tuh, Ka-a-t, kat."

While it's true that the last two decades of schooling have seen a wider use of real books and a greater emphasis on student writing, it's still widely believed that school learning is first a matter of learning the requisite skills needed to read, write, do math and so on. In a very real sense, learning the three R's isn't *doing* "readin', writin', and 'rithmetic" but learning *how* to do them. For purposes of instruction, reading is reduced to learning discrete skills like letter sounds, sound blending and sight vocabulary. Writing is reduced to learning spelling, punctuation and grammar. Mathematics is broken down into various arithmetic operations (addition and multiplication). Even social studies is reduced to a collection of facts to be memorized (like, *What are the chief exports of Argentina?*).

Almost all students will be exposed to skills instruction, but for academically successful students the drill and practice of discrete skills is only one facet of their school experience. For most children who struggle in school, however, the practice of breaking down instruction into a series of small, discrete steps will be the predominant, perhaps even the exclusive, approach. It is reasoned that such students need a program of structured, step-by-step instruction to ensure their success. They won't be able to move forward until they've mastered the basics.

Carolyn's teacher honestly believes that Carolyn will benefit from barking out sounds. She also believes that Carolyn won't be able to enjoy real books on cats, like Bernard Waber's *Rich Cat, Poor Cat* with its genuine human drama and its clever use of repetitive cadences. But from many sources we now know that Carolyn will relish not only the story, but also its clever use of language. In fact, if the teacher reads the story to Carolyn three or four times she'll never have trouble instantly recognizing the word *cat* wherever it might pop up.

Is her teacher actually making reading easier for

Carolyn? We often believe that learning is easier if new things are introduced slowly and in small steps. But although this may apply to some kinds of learning, we now recognize that for much of learning, including reading and writing, breaking it down into bite-sized chunks actually makes it harder.

"When two vowels go walking the first does the talking." Most of us were taught this familiar rule in school. It's the phonics rule I remember best. Just in case you've forgotten how the rule works, let me refresh your memory. When you encounter two vowels together, like the *ea* in *seat* or the *oa* in *boat*, the first vowel makes the sound and the second vowel is silent. Also, the presence of the second vowel often tells the reader that the first vowel is long. For example, in *bet* the vowel is short and in *beat* the vowel is long.

On the surface this seems to be a helpful rule and I've seen it posted in many primary classrooms. But there are problems with it — in fact, it really doesn't work very well. First of all, knowing that the first vowel "does the talking" doesn't tell you whether the first vowel should be long (as in *boat* or *teak*) or short (as in *bread, laugh* or *bought*). Moreover, there are many cases where the first vowel doesn't "do the talking" *(break, beige, chief, country, friend, because)*.

The problem is, this rule works less than half the time, and other phonics rules don't work much better! Few work more than fifty percent of the time. Phonics is simply not a very reliable system, and reading would be an almost impossible task if we had to rely exclusively on it.

In practice, most of us don't have any trouble reading precisely because, as readers, we don't rely *just* on phonics to make sense of print. We always read in context, and the context provides lots of other information to make meaning. We combine our sense of text (*Once upon a time* won't likely be the opening line of a sci-fi novel), our background knowledge, and our knowledge of how language works with what we know about the sounds of letters and combinations of letters to make sense of the printed word. Phonics rules work pretty well *if* we don't focus on them too much.

However, tunnel vision prevents us from remembering this fact. We decide that what ails children who don't do well in school is their lack of basic skills. So we adopt a strategy of focussing on teaching those basic skills: we teach them phonics rules. Then we listen to a relatively poor reader struggling to sound out words in isolation and conclude that the struggle is caused by the student's lack of phonics skills. So we make more plans to emphasize phonics instruction! Conversely, when we listen to the fluent oral reading of a good reader, we cite that student's mastery of phonics skills as the source of his success.

But the real problem isn't the first group's lack of phonics skills and the second group's mastery of them. The problem is that the task of reading through phonics only is almost impossible. Phonics rules just don't work well in isolation. The key to successful reading is the presence of that meaningful context that makes phonics skills work. Good stories, rich language, supportive and enriching illustrations, peer group support, encouragement of risk taking, expectation of meaning — these are the context that makes for good reading. And these are what our tunnel vision encourages us to eliminate from the education of those students who need them most.

I've already pointed out that children who don't do well in school are more likely to be subjected to stripped down skills teaching than other children. This is done with every good intention. Teachers want to make learning easier for less successful students, so they break it down into what they believe are manageable chunks. But meaning always makes learning easier, and decontextualizing learning will always detract from meaning. Instead of breaking learning down into bite-sized chunks, we ought to enrich the learning environment of those children who aren't always successful in school.

For slow readers, teachers focus on letters, letter sounds and words in isolation. What they should do is provide more access to good books, more reading aloud, more authentic children's writing, more language sharing, more risk taking — in short, more opportunities for those children to use many clues rather than only the letters and what they think they know of their sounds. And similar arguments apply to other areas of the curriculum. In math, the emphasis for less successful students tends to be on the rote learning of math facts (3+7=10). But teaching facts in isolation, cut apart from those meaningful contexts in which arithmetic is a tool for solving a real problem (making change, deciding how much wallpaper to purchase), makes arithmetic essentially meaningless, and therefore very difficult to learn.

> The students in one grade two class were all believed to be behind in reading. Each day the reading period began the same way. The teacher gave the students a worksheet so they could practice some phonetic skill. This day's worksheet featured a series of pictures. Next to each picture was a box. The students' task was to put the letter representing the initial sound in the box next to each word. For example, in the box next to the picture of the bird, students were expected to write *b*.

> The children were very noisy while they worked on their worksheets and, in the words of the teacher, "lots of kids were off task." She said that many of the students in her class, especially the boys, had difficulty "getting down to business." Starting the day with worksheets, she believed, would give them the structure they needed to help them settle down.

I detect at least two questionable assumptions in what this teacher believed: that her students were unusually distractible, and that a structured task could help to harness their attention. Lots of people share these two assumptions.

Many children who don't do well in school are inattentive. This is one of the reasons they don't do well.

The idea that attention is a skill that some children have and others don't has always puzzled me. It just doesn't fit my experiences with children. I've never met a child who isn't *ever* able to focus his or her attention. Children wouldn't learn anything at all if they didn't regularly fix their attention on what's going on around them. Even two-year-olds, famous for their distractibility, are able to sustain their attention for considerable periods of time. When he was two, Ian would play with his trucks for over an hour, and he'd be content to sit and watch the neighborhood boys play baseball all afternoon. It isn't that two-year-olds are less able to pay attention than anyone else, it's just that fewer things will hold their attention.

What I'm suggesting here is that the ability of all children (and adults) to fix and sustain their attention is a function of the task they are attending to. If they're interested, they pay attention; if they're not interested, they get distracted.

Since highly structured tasks limit what a child has to attend to at any one time, they are a desirable remedy for attention problems.

As a result of this second assumption, children who don't do well in school are often fed a diet of drills and worksheets which have no inherent meaning and hold no interest for them. Hence they are easily distracted — as we all are with similar tasks. For a summer job I once had to put the same seal on the same ball bearing for eight hours a day. I was fired after a few weeks for talking too much. The mindless task just couldn't hold my attention.

I don't for a minute doubt that some children who struggle in school are easily distracted and often inattentive. But the problem is tedious, boring and meaningless tasks that are incapable of holding their attention. All children can fix and hold their attention if they find a task meaningful and interesting to them. If we find that our students are easily distracted, we should question the ability of the task to grab and hold their attention, not the students' ability to attend.

> The remedial reading teacher was working with Angela, a first grade student. While the teacher did oral reading with another student, Angela was given a worksheet with about 15 pictures on it. Her job was to circle the pictures that began with the *d* sound. She got several wrong — she failed to circle the duck, the donkey and the dish — and the teacher marked these items with a red X. When Angela showed the worksheet at home that night, her mother pointed to the items she'd gotten wrong and asked Angela what they were pictures of. Angela responded, "A bird, a horse and a plate."

This example shows how, for the student, worksheets are filled with meaningless bits and pieces. Meaninglessness is deliberate! The view is that if meaning is removed the student can more easily focus on the skill. But stripping the meaning away from the task makes it more difficult, and often confusing. In this example, the little girl's problem isn't with initial sounds, it's with the pictures. She keeps attributing meaning (we humans always do!), but the meaning she attributes is not the same as the meaning the teacher wants — or the teacher's teaching guide has told her to want.

Successful students probably approach a task like this by looking at each picture and asking themselves, "Could this possibly be a picture of anything which starts with the letter *d*?" Angela, on the other hand, seemed to ask herself first, "What is this a picture of?" and then, "Does it begin with the letter *d*?"

The teachers with whom I work often discover that the problem for many students who don't do well in school isn't lack of basic skills, but difficulty figuring out how to complete the worksheets their teachers give them to teach the skills. Arguably, part of the difference between successful and less successful students is that good students are better able to figure out the task their teachers want them to do. But is that the basis on which we want to make judgments about our students? (In passing we note that there's nothing wrong with Angela's ability to think for herself!)

> Jason didn't do well in math. In particular, he had trouble recalling his math facts. Each day while the other students worked on their math problems, he used a computer program that drilled him on his addition and subtraction facts.
>
> Paul and Adam took turns showing each other the 20 flash cards, each featuring a different word (*make, bike, had*).

Drills and worksheets are a daily fact of school life for most North American school children. But for students who sometimes struggle in school, skills practice is often done at the expense of other, richer opportunities. While low achievers are being drilled on phonics skills, more successful students are reading books. While students who struggle with math spend much (maybe most) of their time learning math facts, more successful students are solving meaningful math problems.

By being exposed to meaningful reading, writing and mathematics, "good" students discover personal reasons for school learning, reasons that connect with their lives outside school. Low achievers can find no personal motivation for learning fragmented skills presented through drill and practice, other than wanting to please their teachers and parents. For these students, reading, writing and arithmetic risk becoming school skills with no meaning for their lives outside of school. By feeding them a steady diet of meaningless drills and exercises, we risk their concluding that all of school is meaningless.

There's an even more important issue here. Many educators now believe that children can only learn to read by reading (real books), to write by writing (meaningful stuff), to do math by doing mathematics (not just arithmetic computations). If this is true — and I believe it is — then students whose instruction focusses on the drilling of skills have fewer opportunities to participate in important learning experiences. They learn skills, but they may not learn to read, write or do math.

My argument here is that our tendency to present

fragmented, decontextualized learning tasks to less successful students (in whom we've already lost faith) makes learning more difficult for them. This automatically contributes extra evidence to our perception that these students are generally less competent. And that, in turn, makes us turn even further away from the kind of education they really need in order to be able to learn — a vicious circle.

A 2.4 reading level

> Stephanie's parents met with the psychologist and the special education teacher, who shared the results of the tests they'd given Stephanie: *Stephanie is a pleasant child who has a Verbal IQ of 90, a Performance IQ of 110, and a Full Scale IQ of 100. She has difficulty in the area of auditory perception; visual perception is a strength. Her performance on a test of receptive vocabulary is similar to that of children several years younger than her. Her reading level is 2.4 . . .*

In our highly technological society we have been led to expect technical solutions to our problems. We take our problem car to a mechanic, expecting him to pinpoint the source of the problem and repair or replace the appropriate parts. When we're sick we go to the doctor, assuming she'll be able to diagnose our ailment and prescribe a remedy. For every problem we've come to expect a relatively straightforward cure. How could we not expect the same thing from our schools? And our schools have sought to satisfy our expectations by identifying students' learning problems and prescribing cures.

There's nothing remarkable about Stephanie's story. Schools commonly respond to children's learning problems with a battery of tests. They probe students' reading, writing, math, language and intelligence, usually with tests in which both the administration and scoring of test items have been standardized to protect them from the intrusion of subjective judgments.

You might say that these tests protect us from

ourselves. We place more faith in them than in our own observations or the observations of parents. A very good, very caring teacher I knew in Green Bay, Wisconsin, changed her mind about a child she'd worked with for almost a year as a result of a test that took less than an hour for the school psychologist to administer. And I've often seen the observations of parents dismissed because they conflicted with the results of the tests.

We place considerable value on standardized tests. They are the basis for many educational decisions, including decisions for special class placement. We hold them in such high esteem because we believe they are objective, uncontaminated by human emotion. But is it possible, or even desirable, to create situations devoid of human feelings?

> Several years ago I worked in a children's diagnostic clinic. Parents brought their children to be tested by a team of professionals, including a pediatrician, a speech pathologist, a social worker, a psychologist and a special educator. After all the testing had been done, the team of professionals met to discuss the child's problem. I once suggested that the parents should be included in this meeting and was flabbergasted by the intense negative reaction to what I considered a reasonable suggestion. My colleagues argued that parents would be too emotional and that this would interfere with the team's discussions.

In the Western world we venerate objectivity and are suspicious of human feelings. We've come to believe that it's possible to separate emotion from our decisions. But we can't do it. It makes no sense to expect that we can separate our decisions from what we are — human. Being human, any decision we make will have an emotional component to it. That's not a weakness, that's simply the way it is. The instruments we use to test students in our schools are chosen on the basis of some feeling (Which is the best test?). Subjective judgments affect someone's decisions about the content of each test. And every test must be interpreted by someone, subjectively.

Making decisions about the kinds of students I've been talking about is a source of anguish to everyone: parents, teachers and students. No teacher wants to tell parents their child isn't doing well. And, of course, no parent or student wants to hear it. Our natural disinclination for telling parents bad news is part of what attracts us to the formal, "objective" process we commonly use for evaluating students. We believe, for example, that standardized tests spare us from some of the pain of telling parents their child isn't doing well. After all, we're just passing along what the tests have told us.

The problem is that these formal tests don't meet the needs of our students. So-called objective measurements, which discount the background and feelings of parents, students and teachers, create a highly artificial context, one very different from the real world where emotions are important factors in human behavior. If schools are going to help students who don't do well, they must allow human emotion.

> Karen knows her daughter Michelle is having trouble learning to read in first grade. She worries a lot about this and sometimes has dreams in which teachers tell her Michelle is retarded. Karen worries that she isn't a good (enough) mother. She also worries that her daughter's problems in school can be traced to a single episode of smoking marijuana when she was pregnant.

Problems in school can be a tragedy for parents. Parents of children who struggle in school feel anxious, fearful, even guilty. And these normal human feelings can drive a wedge between parents and their children, between husbands and wives. And bad feelings, once engendered, spread.

The trouble lies in the ways in which we respond to children's learning problems. We forget that little Stephanie, who has a 2.4 reading level, is somebody's child, somebody's pride and joy. We forget that Stephanie herself has feelings, interests, hopes and fears. We can't really hope to help Stephanie, or others like her, until we recognize that they are people, not grade or age equivalents.

> Betty Schultz did testing for a private school for students with learning disabilities in Cincinnati. It was part of Betty's job to let parents know if she felt their children had a learning disability. If she had bad news she would take a box of tissues to the meeting, because often the parents would cry. And more often than not she would join them and cry too.

Betty didn't sacrifice her objectivity or her integrity by acknowledging the parents' feelings and empathizing with them. Instead, she recognized that decisions can't be made solely on the basis of test scores. Human emotions count too.

We want schooling to affect people's lives, but schools won't be relevant unless we consider the emotions which are also a part of their lives. As teachers, we must remember our own feelings as parents and accept that all parents will respond with strong emotions to any problems their children have.

> Erin Murphy goes to school in a district that requires students to be formally identified as exceptional before they receive any sort of remedial assistance. This is unusual in Ontario, so Erin's mother and father met with school officials to express their concern about the policy. They were worried about the effect a label would have on their daughter's self-esteem and social relationships. The officials told Mr. and Mrs. Murphy there was no reason to worry. If they accepted their daughter's label, so would she.

Presumably if Erin didn't accept her problem, it would be her parents' fault! Yet by taking this stand, the educators were ignoring not only the parents' emotions but also Erin's own emotions and the way they would be affected by those of her parents.

I was presenting to a group of parents and teachers in West Des Moines, Iowa. During a question and answer period, the mother of a twelve-year-old girl with learning disabilities explained to me how she tried to work with her daughter's reading every night. But, she said, whenever she read with her daughter the result was a bitter fight. Her husband, on the other hand, was able to do it without any problems. The mother asked me what she should do. I suggested that she stop reading with her daughter, at least for the time being.

We can so easily become consumed by our children's learning problems. When we look at "problem" children we no longer see them as the children we love and care for, the children who so often surprise us with their intelligence and trust. Instead, the problems the school has pointed out become the focus of our interactions with them. Our warm, playful interactions are replaced by obsessions to "help" and "fix." We worry more about their future and enjoy them less right now. In a very real sense we lose these children to their problems in school. And inevitably the children will begin to see themselves as problems. That can only have serious consequences for their emotional well-being and academic future. In the worst case, their self-respect will be replaced by a fixation on their (even occasional) school failure.

The great emphasis we place on objectivity in the processes through which learning problems are identified and remediated encourages us to forget the obvious: children, teachers and parents are emotional, subjective human beings. Cutting children up into a collection of test scores blinds us to this, leaves us no reason to wonder about the effects of human emotion on learning, and clouds the humanness of our children — their interests, their hopes and their fears. Ultimately, reliance on test scores denies what we are and what our students are: people in whom rational thought, emotion and intuition are inextricably linked. Schools *are* full of emotions, feelings and subjectivity, and if school authorities don't legitimize the healthy kinds, the unhealthy ones will replace them. We shouldn't be suspicious of people whose judgments are affected by their feelings. We should mistrust those who claim that anything else is possible.

How can we help children succeed?

All teachers and parents want the best for children, including those who are less successful. If children struggle in school, we go out of our way to help them. Our culture has committed considerable human and economic resources to solving the problems of children who fail in school.

Unfortunately, there are ample reasons to doubt the success of our efforts. I must emphasize that the problem isn't teachers — almost all the teachers I've ever known are warm, caring and dedicated professionals. The fly in the ointment, as I've tried to show in the first part of this book, is the process by which we respond to children's learning problems.

Our almost singleminded focus on children's problems has blinded us to their marvellous accomplishments. We pay far less attention to what children *can* do than to what they can't do. Lacking faith in their ability to learn, we deliberately fragment learning in an honest effort to make it easier, only to find that we've made it harder instead. Our efforts to create an objective process for identifying children's learning problems have unintentionally created a process stripped of human emotion, one that is insensitive to the feelings of parents, teachers and students and that can, in fact, be detrimental. There are good reasons to feel that, in the case of children who struggle in school, our solution has become part of the problem.

There is an alternative to the fragmented, decontextualized (behavioral) approach to teaching and learning that has dominated education, in particular that of students who don't always do well. I don't intend to offer here specific advice for constructing lessons. Instead, I want to discuss the general principles I believe should guide the instruction of all children. If our traditional responses to learning problems are inadequate, how should we respond instead? How can we best encourage learning in all children, regardless of their apparent ability or lack of it? How should we go about challenging all children to simply do what they do best — learn?

Faith

I once heard a story about an eight-year-old boy named Albert who attended a school for learning disabled students. Albert did little reading or writing and seemed incapable of doing even the simplest addition and subtraction. Quite by chance his teacher discovered that at home Albert kept complete statistics on all his favorite baseball players, regularly computing their batting averages and earned run averages.

Margaret Slade teaches a tenth grade basic writing class in the Toronto area. She tells the story about one of the boys in her class who blamed his writing difficulties on the fact that he "didn't know anything." Shortly after he told her this she discovered that his art was being exhibited in a special one-man show.

When Bryant Fillion was a professor at the Ontario Institute for Studies in Education, he told the story of a ninth grade student he'd worked with when he was a classroom teacher, a boy he believed to be illiterate. The day after he announced a short-story writing contest to his class, this student handed him a short story. Professor Fillion asked the student where the story had come from and the boy said, "I have a trunk full of them at home." Apparently this "illiterate" boy was writing short stories on his own at home — stories so good, in fact, that the one he shared with his teacher won a prize in an international short-story competition.

These stories reveal the talents of three students who didn't do well in school. It would be easy to argue, I suppose, that these students are exceptional. It's true that most students who don't do well in school aren't gifted artists, writers or mathematicians. But all children who have difficulty getting along in school share one accomplishment no less remarkable than the achievements of these three students: except for the most severely retarded, all of them, including those who have experienced repeated school failure, have learned language.

This extraordinary feat — learning to talk (or sign, in the case of some hearing impaired children) — is the supreme evidence of children's intelligence. Within a few short years after their birth, children learn thousands of words. They also learn rules for combining words into sentences, rules which are of bewildering complexity. And they learn how to use what they know about language appropriately in social contexts. Children learn all this without explicit instruction. I believe that learning language is the most remarkable human achievement, and the best evidence for the intelligence of all human beings.

At heart this book contains a simple plea: we must believe that all our students can learn. The achievement of language gives us evidence of their amazing learning ability, but it isn't the only evidence. All children, even those who haven't done well in school and those we believe have had limited experience, know many things. They know about sports and TV, pets and dinosaurs, foods and fashion, getting along in their communities. In short, they know a great deal about the world in which they live. The question for some children isn't whether or not they learn, but whether or not (and what) they learn *in school*. Children are always learning. It's just that they don't always learn what we adults want them to learn at the time and in the form we want them to learn it.

All children are born intelligent, although they are not all intelligent in the same way. Not all children will excel in school, but all are capable of learning there. Believing that students can learn encourages us to look for evidence that they have learned. Instead of asking questions like, "Can they read or write?" or "Do they know anything about math or history?" we'll ask, "*What* do they know about reading, writing, math or history?"

Rather than focussing on what our students don't know, we must focus on what they do know, on the intellectual, social and language resources they bring to school. This is the foundation upon which we can build. Believing that children can learn won't solve all their problems, but believing that they can't may guarantee that school will be a struggle for them.

The following story was written by Ellen, a seven-year-old student in a class for students with learning disabilities.

One Halloween Nit
I cam to a Homt house
I Noxt on Thedor
and a Sklt open et
I run to My house
and I lokt My dor
and I et My cand
and I Wit TY

Ellen's story has no punctuation; she doesn't always use standard English grammar; almost one third of the words she has written are misspelled. But this analysis of Ellen's writing, although not inaccurate, is misleading. It ignores what Ellen does know.

Take spelling. Although nearly a third of Ellen's words are spelled incorrectly, over two thirds are spelled correctly. And even her errors demonstrate her considerable knowledge of letter-sound correspondences in written English. Her spelling mistakes are not random strings of letters. All of her misspellings are attempts to represent words phonetically; it's her misfortune that many English words can't *be* represented phonetically. When she uses a phonetic strategy for spelling she represents all *(nakt, lakt, cand)* or most *(sklt, wit)* of the sounds in the word. In the case of *dor* she uses a strategy that reflects her knowledge of conventional English spelling *(d* plus *or)*. So it's not that Ellen doesn't know how to spell. At this stage of her development she simply over-relies on phonetic spellings. In time, as she gains more experience with print, she, like other children, will learn more and more conventional spellings.

Teachers must become "kidwatchers," as Yetta Goodman suggests, constantly looking for evidence of children's learning. When they do, they are often surprised at what they discover. When Judy Mullen, one of my Masters students, studied the language her students used as they worked at the computer, she discovered that it was much more sophisticated than she had expected. Until she watched carefully, she didn't realize how much her students knew.

If we trust children's ability to learn, and if we observe them as they read, write, compute and respond to instruction, we'll discover that what they know is often much beyond their performance as matched to some (arbitrary) adult standard. And if we trust their ability to learn, we're much more likely to create opportunities for them to show us what they know.

Meaning

When my daughter Anne was almost five years old she still hadn't memorized her phone number. We live in a very large city, so my wife and I were concerned. Each day we drilled her on it. We even tried to put our phone number to music, but nothing seemed to work. One day I asked Anne why she couldn't learn her phone number. She told me, "I'm not going to get lost."

Several months later Anne asked if her friend Marla could stay for dinner. We said that it was okay with us but first Marla had to call her mom and ask permission. Marla went to the phone and started dialing her number. Seeing this, Anne asked Marla if she knew her phone number, and Marla nodded yes. Anne then asked me what our number is and I told her. She's never forgotten it.

Like Anne, all of us learn best (and often without much effort) what is personally important to us. Seven meaningless numbers are hard to memorize, but few of us have any difficulty learning the telephone number of a friend. Almost everyone in Toronto knows the phone number for the city's largest pizza delivery chain — useful information for a pizza lover like me! And which of us hasn't heard a story about a student whose reading got a sudden boost when he or she began preparing to take the written driver's test? Personally I find it impossible to learn to make simple repairs to my car or house, largely, I'm sure, because I'm not very interested in learning those things. Learning what is neither interesting nor important to us isn't impossible; all of us have done it. But it is much more difficult.

There's no reason why schools can't be important and interesting places for students — often, they already are. But routine drills and the practicing of basic skills are never going to be interesting. Skills can be dressed up in glitzy programs or kits to make them fun, but that's an admission that what we're teaching doesn't have the potential to excite children's interest. There's no reason why school learning shouldn't be potentially meaningful to students and able to excite their interest. Reading, writing, math, science and social studies have the potential to affect children's lives by fulfilling their need to communicate and to make sense of their world. If what we teach seems boring and uninteresting, the problem may not be what we teach but how we teach it.

> Nine-month-old Ian sits at the breakfast table with his sister and parents. Ian begins to cry. His mother asks him what he wants. Does he want toast? Does he want more cereal? More milk? With each question Ian cries harder, and he ends up throwing his bowl of cereal on the floor. Finally his mother asks him if he wants some juice. Ian nods his head and stops crying. Less than a year later, under roughly the same conditions, Ian holds up his cup and says, "Juice, pease." Immediately his father gets him some juice.

Children learn language because it works, because it's a powerful tool for getting things done. It's the power of language to influence people to provide various goods and services that motivates small children to learn to talk. The praise and rewards of parents, however desirable, play only a minor role in language learning. Similarly, children learn about the world around them because this knowledge protects them and satisfies their natural curiosity.

In short, learning is functional. Outside school, people learn best and most easily when learning fulfills some personal need. School learning is no different. Reading, writing, math, science, social studies and so on have excellent potential to fulfill personal needs. Given the right conditions, students can discover that school learning has something in it for them personally. They'll learn in school because, like learning to talk, it works.

Anthropologist Shirley Brice Heath reports that in the relatively poor black families she studied in the Piedmont region of the southeastern United States, children as young as four years old were able to scan the price tags of items at the grocery store and pick out the price. Later, children were expected to be able to remember prices from week to week and to make comparisons when shopping at the supermarket.

In the community she describes, children learn fairly sophisticated math skills at a surprisingly early age in order to protect their families from high prices. What we teach in our classrooms also has the potential to fulfill important personal needs in our students' lives long after they leave school. Reading, for example, isn't just a school skill. It's a means of getting information, a way of communicating with other people, and a source of pleasure. Writing functions as a memory aid, a medium for communication and a means of self-expression. Even subjects like social studies can help students get along by improving their understanding of the world in which they live.

Unfortunately, for many students, especially those for whom school is a struggle, reading, writing, math, science and social studies seem to be only school skills, with little relevance to their lives outside of school. Our ways of teaching these subjects often give students little motivation to learn. We need to create school environments that allow students to discover that school learning has the potential to fulfill important personal needs in their lives outside of school.

I don't mean that we should actively try to convince students that what we're teaching is important. I don't think we'll get very far merely lecturing to them that if they don't do well in school they won't get good jobs or go to college. That kind of payoff is too distant. But if we don't fragment learning, then we make it possible for children to discover for themselves that school learning has something in it for them — in the present as well as in the difficult-for-them-to-imagine future.

> Jane teaches in an inner-city primary level class for students with learning disabilities in Denver, Colorado. When students enter Jane's classroom, the first thing they see is the daily lunch menu posted in front of the doorway. Separate schedules for the day and the month are posted in the same area. Several commercial book posters are displayed throughout the room. Each student's name and a brief biographical sketch are written on a chart and posted on one wall. Jane has copied and illustrated six Shel Silverstein poems on large pieces of tagboard, and these are displayed around the room. Her students' written work is displayed under the chalkboard at the front of the room. A bookcase in the middle of the room contains nearly 100 books for the students to read. Each day Jane selects one of these books to read to her class.

The print in Jane's classroom functions a lot like that in the demonstration booths at a home show my wife Chris and I attended last year. It included over twenty booths where people were demonstrating various gadgets designed to make housework easier. The people selling these products obviously felt that it wasn't enough just to show their products, they also had to demonstrate them. Presumably if people saw how the gadgets worked and how useful they could be in their homes, they would be more likely to buy them.

The presence of meaningful print in Jane's class demonstrated to the children what reading is for (to inform, entertain, communicate) and how it works. It also shows them how important reading is to Jane. And, like the demonstrators at the home show, Jane hopes that when her students discover how useful reading is, they'll try it out for themselves.

Other teachers provide similarly powerful demonstrations for their students. The presence of a store in a first grade classroom encourages children to discover personal uses for math. A map of the neighborhood around the school, drawn by a group of fourth grade students, demonstrates the relevance of social studies. A ninth grade history teacher who begins the year by having his students research their family histories and construct family trees demonstrates the utility of the historical method.

The trick is to provide meaningful demonstrations of real reading, writing, science, math and social studies. We want to entice students to discover that school learning has meaning for them in their daily lives, both in and out of school. It's hard to convince them of that by telling them explicitly; we must create conditions that encourage them to discover it on their own. How? By creating an environment that demonstrates to them what we're trying to teach, and shows them the potential meaning of school learning for them personally. We shouldn't try to tell them; we should show them.

Invitations

There were several learning centers around Mrs. Paul's third grade classroom. These were usually tables containing objects or materials Mrs. Paul hoped would engage her students' interest and encourage learning. One center contained colored markers and strips of tagboard. Above the table hung a picture of a car with a bumper sticker. At another center the teacher had placed pens, pencils and a pad of lined paper with *TO:* and *FROM:* printed on each sheet. Next to the table were cubbyholes, each hole labeled with the name of a student. At the third center Mrs. Paul had placed several collections of children's poetry. A tape recorder was also available so students could listen to some of the poems Mrs. Paul had recorded on tape. A pad of lined paper, some drawing paper, and a variety of pens, pencils, markers and crayons were also left at the center in the hope that children would make drawings to go with their favorite poems or perhaps even try to write poems of their own. Mrs. Paul encouraged her students to visit the centers and gave them time to do so. She did not, however, tell the students what they were to do at the centers beyond visiting them.

When we issue an invitation we seek someone's voluntary participation. An invitation can take the form of a formal request, like an invitation to a birthday party, or it can take the form of a wink or a beckoning finger. The presence of interesting objects or materials may also be inviting. Teachers who fill their classrooms with print invite their students to read. The strategic placement of rulers, tape measures, measuring cups and scales invites students to make measurements. Teachers who place pencil and paper by the resource books invite students to take notes.

Interesting activities invite students to share and discuss. I once taped groups of students working with a computer software program that enabled them to draw anything they wished, and in color. In over an hour of taping I observed students sharing, speculating and planning without a single "off-task" utterance. Meaningful activities have the power to hold students' attention for extended periods of time and invite useful talk. In general, teachers whose classrooms are interesting places invite students to do interesting things.

The power of invitations depends on their ability to engage and sustain children's attention and interest. Glitzy programs and kits may invite children's participation, but only personally meaningful and relevant activities will sustain their interest. Children (and adults) learn by doing, not by learning how. Invitations are important because they are teachers' primary means to get students to participate. We cannot coerce students into participating. Their participation is something we can only encourage, not require.

Mandated participation encourages passive acquiescence. Demanding that students "pay attention," for example, encourages them to put on attending behaviors — to look as if they're paying attention. Demanding that students read or write may encourage them to look as if they're reading or writing, but it's easy to discover that they take no personal ownership of the reading or writing they do on demand.

Of course, it takes interesting things to invite students' participation. Teachers must work hard to keep their classrooms interesting places that appeal to the questions and experiences students bring to school. Interesting materials and activities will excite children's natural curiosity, but they lose the ability to interest as their novelty wears off. For example, a dinosaur display may excite interest, inviting students to talk, read and write about dinosaurs. But after a while any display, no matter how exciting initially, will lose its power and become background only. In many of the primary classrooms I visit, the print around the classroom loses its power to invite reading long before it's refreshed.

The manner of an invitation is especially important. A first grade teacher I know has such deep affection for the books she shares with her students that there's no mistaking the genuineness of her invitation to her students. Conversely, I recall a student teacher who began a poetry unit with a class of seventh graders by confessing, "I don't like poetry, but . . ." This is much like a car salesman who begins his sales pitch by listing the car's faults. We may give him credit for his honesty, but we're not likely to buy anything from him. If students reject our invitations, it may be time to consider the possibility that our solicitations aren't inviting enough.

Trust

> When Anne was four years old she once complained
> to her mother that I was "harassing" her because I
> wouldn't let her go swimming. Three years later she
> asked me to get our dog out from under my desk by
> "harassing" it.

Errors play an important role in learning. Like little
scientists, children try out their knowledge of language
and the world around them, in part to help them make
sense of things. For example, children try out words to test
their meaning. Anne's understanding of the word "harass"
certainly evolved over three years, even though the
meaning she attributes to the word is still a bit different
from its conventional meaning. By using the word she is
gradually getting control of its meaning.

> At seven years, Anne wrote a sympathy card for her
> mother after she had burned her hand and her lip.

I hope your hand feels better and your lip.

As with spoken language, children learn about writing and spelling by trying out written words. When Anne's mother received the sympathy card, she thanked Anne for her concern and congratulated her on her effort. Of course this made Anne very proud, but it also encouraged future efforts. That same night she wrote five or six more notes to her mother. Had we chosen instead to correct Anne's spelling, we might have discouraged future experimentation and, inadvertently, interfered with her learning. Why not take heart when we see children being willing to risk mistakes? It's only through their mistakes that their hypotheses about the world evolve.

It is children's willingness to try things out and risk errors that accounts for their remarkable learning ability. If we encourage them to try, they are completely unabashed about it. Adults, on the other hand, are often reluctant to risk mistakes for fear of looking foolish. This reluctance is part of the reason why second language learning is much more difficult for adults than for children. Similarly, children who have learned to play it safe, who are unwilling to risk errors, whose experiences have taught them perhaps to fear failure, give themselves fewer opportunities to learn, and contribute to their own learning problems.

> The students in a seventh grade classroom had just finished their daily silent reading time with books of their own choosing. The teacher, Linda, began asking them to talk about what they'd been reading. When she saw the book Mark was reading she said, "Mark, I see you're reading another one of those gory books. What do you see in them?" Mark gave a lengthy, honest response to Linda's question.

I'm always encouraging teachers to increase the amount of talk in their classrooms and, of course, one way to get students to talk is by asking good questions. When I heard Mark's extended response to Linda's question I thought I had an example of an excellent question that I could share with other teachers. But when I considered the matter more carefully I realized there wasn't anything remarkable about the question itself. Mark could just as easily have replied, "I just like them." No, something else was important here.

I now understand that Mark gave a detailed and forthright response to Linda's question because he believed that Linda was honestly interested in what he had to say. This atmosphere of trust, of knowing that the teacher really cared about what her students had to say, had to have been nurtured over a period of time. Freed from the tyranny of routine evaluation and the pressures of "getting it right," Mark and the other students in Linda's class willingly shared, speculated and hypothesized — all important elements in their learning.

I often see the converse of this healthy situation. In many classrooms students are unwilling to take chances and risk mistakes because of the certainty of evaluation, and the chance that they might be "wrong." We must remember that all of us, children and adults, learn best in an atmosphere of trust, free from anxiety and the tyranny of inevitable evaluation.

Teachers provide the conditions for learning. Teachers can, and should, challenge students to consider alternative hypotheses (including those of the teacher), but within an atmosphere in which honest sharing and speculating are encouraged. They can do that by personally challenging students to consider or reconsider their theories of the world. They can also encourage discussions that will present students with differing points of view. Or they can expand background knowledge, which then may influence students to re-evaluate their views. The key here is that teachers must challenge students to learn and grow, without telling them whether they are right or wrong in terms of some subjective adult standard. Challenging students encourages learning; telling them that they are wrong discourages it.

Connections

Anne Drummond taught a third grade class in a multi-ethnic school in Toronto. The day I visited, she read aloud *The Snow Queen* by Hans Christian Andersen. Before she read the story to her class she held up the book, showed her students the cover and asked them, "What do you think this is a picture of?" After some discussion there seemed to be agreement that this was a picture of the Snow Queen. Anne asked them if they had read any other books about the Snow Queen. Some of them had. Next she told the class that this book had been written by Hans Christian Andersen and asked if they'd read any other stories by that author. They had, and another brief discussion followed. Finally, she paged through the book, showing the class the pictures and inviting them to predict what the story was going to be about.

People learn against a background of experience. We make sense of the world that surrounds us by connecting new information to our previous experiences. What we learn is dependent on what we already know. My understanding of a screeching sound in my car's engine is different from the understanding an auto mechanic has because our respective experiences with engine trouble are different. We are both able to make sense of the problem, but probably not the same sense. The mechanic may try to explain the problem to me, but my background knowledge limits my ability to see the problem as he or she sees it. Nevertheless, I am able to make some sense of what the mechanic says by drawing on whatever experience I do have with cars (including the fact that the repairs are likely to be expensive!)

The various phenomena our daily lives present to us make sense only if they are relevant to what we already know. Information that doesn't relate to our previous experience is virtually uninterpretable. For example, a lecture on theoretical physics will mean little to me if I lack the relevant background knowledge. Similarly, when fragmented skills are presented abstracted from meaning (which has been deliberately stripped away), students cannot draw on their previous experiences to make sense of them. They can learn only by rote. Of course, it is possible to learn rote skills, but this kind of learning is more difficult and more easily forgotten. I think of a cartoon I saw of two students standing in front of a classroom door with a sign that says *Geography test postponed.* "Darn it," one of the students observes. "Now I have to remember the capitals of the provinces for another week."

What we teach must be potentially meaningful and relevant to our students — it must have the possibility of making sense to them. For example, the content of the physics lecture has the potential for making sense if the lecturer is able to make the necessary connections between what she is saying and what I know, or if she is able to help me build up the relevant background knowledge during her presentation. Similarly, teachers sometimes have to help make connections between the content of their lessons and the students' background knowledge. But these connections are possible only if what's being taught has the potential to make sense.

Anne Drummond spent 20 minutes preparing her students for her reading of *The Snow Queen.* Using discussion as a means of activating her students' relevant background knowledge, she made it easier for them to make sense of the story she would be reading them. Teachers may also have to help students develop relevant background knowledge through the use of presentations, films, relevant readings and field trips, as well as discussion. Again, the assumption is always that what is being taught has the potential to make sense, to be integrated into the students' background knowledge.

Doing, sharing

Every morning Ms. Todd's third grade students spend twenty minutes writing in their journals.

Mr. French brought two chocolate cakes to his second grade class. He asked the students to decide among themselves how the cakes were to be cut.

At Benjamin Franklin Elementary every student reads silently for fifteen minutes after recess.

Mrs. Rohr, a seventh grade history teacher, asked her students to do family trees for their first assignment.

Mr. Daniels had his fifth grade science class spend a period examining and making notes on whatever they found in the vacant lot next to the school.

An old and well accepted principle in education is that children (and adults) learn by doing. Teachers, especially teachers of children who aren't always successful in school, sometimes forget this principle and replace it with an emphasis on *learning how,* in isolation from actually *doing.* Students are asked to learn facts or skills presumed to be relevant to reading, writing, history, math or science, at the expense of doing the things themselves. But in a lot of cases the skills aren't prerequisites at all. Usually children can learn the skills as they do the reading, writing, computing and so on.

Students, all students, should have constant opportunities to practice what it is we want them to learn. They must participate in activities similar to those engaged in by experts. In other words, students must do *real* reading, writing, math, history, science and so on — not just learn how. Students don't learn to do by learning how, they learn how by doing.

Two girls are writing about a cross-country trip as part of a social studies lesson, using a computer simulation:

Teresa (writing): *We would start by selling our fish for their . . .*

Mary: "Their? Who?"

Teresa: "Quebec and Ontario." (She crosses out *their* and writes *Quebec and Ontario,* then continues writing.) . . . *lumber that we* (crosses out *we*) *is greatly needed here. Getting to Saskatchewan, we would sell our fish to them.* "We're getting to B.C. What have they got?" (After some discussion she continues writing.) *Finally, we arrive at B.C. to sell them our potatoes and frozen veggies for some B.C. cedar shakes, and now our journey is done.*

Much of what we learn in our lives we learn from

someone else. And much of what we learn from others we don't learn by being told; we learn by watching and by working together. Cooperation and collaboration play a major role in human learning. For example, our understanding of a story grows as we share it with someone else. As writers we learn about the needs of readers by sharing what we've written and listening to what readers have to say. We learn how to participate in conversations by taking part in real conversations with real people. We test our hypotheses about science, history and geography through discussion with peers, as in the example above. And we often do our best work when we work with other people.

Human knowledge is socially constructed and is learned best in social settings where students can work together. Teachers should construct a community of learners where students are free to learn from each other instead of finding themselves in competition. Working together is not a form of cheating. The best learning environment is a climate of trust where students are confident that both their teachers and their peers will respect what they have to say.

> Seven-year-old Amy has a fluctuating hearing loss which, among other things, interferes with her ability to hear and follow directions from her teacher. Amy's pride prevents her from admitting she has a hearing problem, or ever asking for help. Yet one of the little girls who sits near Amy recognizes her problem and has taken it upon herself to always repeat the teacher's directions to Amy.

> There's a hum of activity in Mr. O'Malley's seventh grade writing class. Several students are sharing what they've written with their classmates, who are responding with helpful advice. One student stops by a friend's desk, reads what he has written, and offers, "That's really good." Another asks a friend how to spell a word. Still another asks several students seated near her what they think about the title she has chosen for her story. Several students discuss potential writing topics. Interestingly, the teacher is

generally unaware of the support his students are
giving to each other.

I believe that children naturally care about other
children and are anxious to support each other. But they
will be able to express their caring for each other only in an
atmosphere of trust, one in which cooperation and
collaboration are stressed. In the example above Mr.
O'Malley may be unaware of the extent of sharing and
support going on in his classroom, but he helped to create
the conditions that encourage it.

Unfortunately, especially for older students, the
emphasis in too many classrooms is on competition, on
getting ahead (of someone else). Doing well in school is
defined not in terms of students' personal
accomplishments, but in terms of their achievements
relative to those of their classmates. Conventional wisdom
has it that competition brings out the best in us. It does in
some people, in some circumstances. But it paralyzes
others. For most, the best they can be is best discovered in
an atmosphere of sharing and collaboration.

Teachers as learners

Mark and his teacher are discussing a report Mark is
writing on the war in Iraq:

Teacher: You're writing about the Persian Gulf. You
probably know about it. I don't. What are you trying
to get across? What do you want me to know?

Teachers promote student learning by creating the
conditions for learning to occur and by providing students
with models of what mature learners do. Teachers are also
fellow collaborators who learn from their students and
support what they are trying to do. In this example the
teacher doesn't tell the student what to write about.
Instead he tries to support what the student is doing by
asking questions that may help clarify the student's
thinking.

I asked the students in my university reading class,
all of whom were teachers, to break into small groups

and discuss the following question: *What is the role of teaching strategies in students' reading and writing development?* As I eavesdropped on the groups, I overheard a teacher named Shari say, "I don't use teaching strategies when I teach reading and writing."

When I asked Shari what she meant by her comment, she told me that she tries to help students as best she can, but because every student is different she's never quite sure what she's going to do when she responds to an individual's reading and writing. What guides her are her instincts about how children learn.

She explained that she does use teaching strategies in the sense that she consciously and deliberately tries to help her students make sense of reading and writing. But she believes that since each child is different, each setting different, and each teacher different, each instructional event must be unique. So she feels no cookbook of educational strategies is possible. She can and does learn from other teachers, and from the books and articles she reads, but these lessons serve only as demonstrations for her. Based on her knowledge and her experiences, she invents strategies or adapts the strategies of others according to her reading of the teaching situation.

I agree with Shari's assessment of the role of teaching strategies. Good teachers are artists who respond creatively to each teaching situation. There isn't a point in the lives of teachers when they've learned *the* way to teach. Teachers are always learning. They are always combining their knowledge and experience with their daily observations of students in their quest for more and better teaching strategies. In a sense, a teacher isn't something one is, but something one is always in the process of becoming.

Teachers learn by teaching and must, therefore, be free to experiment and learn from their mistakes, just like the children they teach. We must give teachers credit for what they know. Only when teachers are seduced by cookbooks, when they stop learning from their students, should we be concerned.

Ms. March is a fourth grade teacher. Each day she reads and writes while her students are reading and writing. When her students have a period of sustained silent reading she reads along with them. During the first fifteen minutes of the daily forty-five minute writing period Ms. March writes. The children know not to bother her during this time. Ms. March regularly reads and writes at home and routinely shares what she's reading and writing with her students. Her students especially enjoy it when she shares poems she has written.

When we read, we do many things to try to make sense of what it is we're reading: predict, reread, skip words or passages, scan, stop and think, perhaps reflect about what we already know. But we don't always do the same things; it depends on what we're reading, our purposes for reading and so on. Similarly, when we write we don't follow a linear process: writing, revising and editing. As I'm writing this book I'm simultaneously creating, revising and editing.

I think it's very difficult, if not impossible, to be an effective teacher of reading or writing without having a fairly good idea of what readers and writers do as they read and write. And I don't think teachers can be told these things. I think they can only learn about the processes of reading and writing by being readers and writers themselves. And even that isn't enough. They must actively reflect on what they do as readers and writers. They must also try to discover what other readers and writers do. All readers and writers don't go about reading and writing in identical ways, so teachers must become aware of the variations within their classrooms.

This means talking with other readers and writers about reading and writing. Teachers need to get together and talk with each other; in fact, some university courses on reading and writing provide opportunities for that. Teachers may also find it helpful to talk about all this with their students.

What's true of reading and writing is just as true of

other areas of the curriculum. To understand what goes on when people do history, math, geography or science, teachers must reflect on it. This doesn't mean that teachers need to have a degree in math or history before they can teach it. We all use methods of history and math in our own lives, often without realizing it. However, few of us reflect on the processes. I plead guilty! The examples I use are always for reading and writing because I've given a great deal of thought to those processes, while I've given very little to the processes of history, math, science or geography. I think one of the reasons that many of us have so much difficulty teaching science is that we don't know or haven't considered what people *do* when they "do" science.

It adds up to this: teachers should be seen to practice what they teach. They should have a clear sense of the processes they wish to encourage in their students, and they should always continue to think and learn, even while they're teaching.

A final word

I'm going to end this book where I started it, reflecting on my own experiences as a teacher of young children, especially my experience at Fair Acres. I recall the assumptions my colleagues and I made about the mentally retarded students we taught, assumptions that affected both how and what we taught them. We believed they couldn't learn to read and write, so we didn't teach reading or writing. We assumed they could learn only basic math skills, so we taught only basic math skills. The fact that they didn't learn much about reading or writing or math only confirmed our assumptions. And even if they did learn to read or write, we didn't give them the opportunity to show us what they knew.

In a way we guaranteed that our students wouldn't learn the things that might convince us they weren't retarded. We didn't make those children retarded, but we failed to challenge them to show us what they could do. When I look back I can't help but feel disappointment. But I don't reproach myself for the way I taught then, any more than I would want teachers to reproach themselves for the mistakes they may have made in the past. I understand that the problem wasn't me, but the behavioral model that guided my teaching. I'm gratified that I've been able to learn from my mistakes. For the sake of my students, I just wish I'd learned a little sooner.

What I wish I had done, what I hope my daughter's teachers will do, what I hope the teachers of any child who doesn't do well in school will do, is to challenge *all* children to learn, by having faith in their natural intelligence and by creating conditions that make it possible for them to take advantage of their remarkable learning ability.

Expect that students will learn, recognize how best to encourage their learning, create conditions that will make learning natural. If we can learn to teach in this way, every child will become a successful learner. It won't be easy, but perhaps we can reduce some of the pain and suffering caused today by school failure. And that will be worth it.

The *Bright Idea* Series

In *Bright Idea* books, gifted authors reveal to readers the hearts of their professional lives. What has excited them professionally? What have they spent their years discovering, and why?

In these books they dress some old truths in new styles, and reveal some new truths about children, about language, about learning, about teachers, teaching and parenting.

The series was conceived and is published in Canada, but the authors come from all over: the United States, New Zealand, The Netherlands, Great Britain, Canada.

So far twelve titles have been published:

☞	**The Craft of Children's Writing**	Judith Newman
	Grand Conversations: **Literature Groups in Action**	Ralph Peterson and Maryann Eeds
	Learning Computer Learning	Veronica Buckley and Martin Lamb
	Other Countries, Other Schools	Mike Bruce
☞	**Reading Begins at Birth**	David B. Doake
☞	**Spel . . . Is a Four-Letter Word**	J. Richard Gentry
	Tests: Marked for Life?	S. Alan Cohen
	The Tone of Teaching	Max van Manen
☞	**What's Whole in Whole Language?**	Ken Goodman
	When School Is a Struggle	Curt Dudley-Marling
☞	**Whole Language: Inquiring Voices**	Dorothy Watson, Carolyn Burke and Jerome Harste
	A Word is a Word . . . Or Is It?	Michael Graves

In Canada, order from Scholastic Canada Ltd., 123 Newkirk Road, Richmond Hill, Ontario L4C 3G5.

In the United States, order from Scholastic Inc., P.O. Box 7502, Jefferson City, MO 65102.

☞ Available in New Zealand and Australia through Ashton Scholastic, and in the United Kingdom through Scholastic Publications.